FIGHTING FOR PEACE

Your Role in a Culture Too Comfortable with Violence

CAROL HOWARD MERRITT
& TYLER WIGG-STEVENSON
RE/FRAME BY STEPHAN JOUBERT

ZONDERVAN

Fighting for Peace
Copyright © 2013 by Barna Group

This title is also available as a Zondervan ebook.
Visit www.zondervan.com/ebooks.

This title is also available in a Zondervan audio edition.
Visit www.zondervan.fm.

Requests for information should be addressed to:

Zondervan, *Grand Rapids, Michigan 49530*

ISBN 978-0-310-43345-3 (softcover)

Published in association with the literary agency of The Fedd Agency, Inc,
401 Ranch Road 620 South, Suite 350c, Austin, TX 78734.

Cover design and interior graphics: Amy Duty
Interior design: Kate Mulvaney

Printed in the United States of America

13 14 15 16 17 18 /DCI/ 18 17 16 15 14 13 12 11 10 9 8 7 6 5 4 3 2 1

CONTENTS

....

WHY YOU NEED FRAMES

These days, you probably find yourself with less time than ever.

Everything seems like it's moving at a faster pace — except your ability to keep up.

Somehow, you are weighed down with more obligations than you have ever had before.

Life feels more complicated. More complex.

If you're like most people, you probably have lots of questions about how to live a life that matters. You feel as though you have more to learn than can possibly be learned. But with smaller chunks of time and more sources of information than ever before, where can you turn for real insight and livable wisdom?

Barna Group has produced this series to examine the complicated issues of life and to help you live more meaningfully. We call it FRAMES — like a good set of eyeglasses that help you see the world more clearly ... or a work of art perfectly hung that invites you to look more closely ... or a building's skeleton, the part that is most essential to its structure.

The FRAMES Season 1 collection provides thoughtful and concise, data-driven and visually appealing insights for anyone who wants a more faith-driven and fulfilling life. In each FRAME we couple new cultural analysis from our team at Barna with an essay from leading voices in the field, providing information and ideas for you to digest in a more easily consumed number of words.

After all, it's a fast-paced world, full of words and images vying for your attention. Most of us have a number of half-read or "read someday" books on our shelves. But each FRAME aims to give you the essential information and real-life application behind one of today's most crucial trends in less than one-quarter the length of most books. These are big ideas in small books—designed so you truly can read less but know more. And the infographics and ideas in this FRAME are intended for share-ability. So read it, then find someone to "frame" with these ideas, and keep the conversation going (see "Share This Frame" on page 89).

Furthermore, each FRAME brings a distinctly Christian point of view to today's trends. In times of uncertainty, people look for guides. And we believe the Christian community is trying to make sense of the dramatic social changes happening around us.

Over the past thirty years, Barna Group has built a reputation as a trusted analyst of religion and culture. We offer cultural discernment for the Christian community by thoughtful analysts who care enough to tell the truth about what's really happening in today's society.

So sit back, but not for long. With FRAMES we invite you to read less and know more.

DAVID KINNAMAN
FRAMES, executive producer
president / Barna Group

ROXANNE STONE
FRAMES, general editor
vice president / Barna Group

Learn more at www.barnaframes.com.

FRAMES

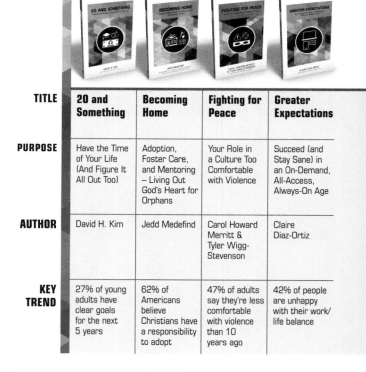

TITLE	20 and Something	Becoming Home	Fighting for Peace	Greater Expectations
PURPOSE	Have the Time of Your Life (And Figure It All Out Too)	Adoption, Foster Care, and Mentoring – Living Out God's Heart for Orphans	Your Role in a Culture Too Comfortable with Violence	Succeed (and Stay Sane) in an On-Demand, All-Access, Always-On Age
AUTHOR	David H. Kim	Jedd Medefind	Carol Howard Merritt & Tyler Wigg-Stevenson	Claire Diaz-Ortiz
KEY TREND	27% of young adults have clear goals for the next 5 years	62% of Americans believe Christians have a responsibility to adopt	47% of adults say they're less comfortable with violence than 10 years ago	42% of people are unhappy with their work/life balance

PERFECT FOR SMALL GROUP DISCUSSION

FRAMES Season 1: DVD
FRAMES Season 1: The Complete Collection

READ LESS.
KNOW MORE.

The Hyperlinked Life	Multi-Careering	Sacred Roots	Schools in Crisis	Wonder Women
Live with Wisdom in an Age of Information Overload	Do Work That Matters at Every Stage of Your Journey	Why the Church Still Matters	They Need Your Help (Whether You Have Kids or Not)	Navigating the Challenges of Motherhood, Career, and Identity
Jun Young & David Kinnaman	Bob Goff	Jon Tyson	Nicole Baker Fulgham	Kate Harris
71% of adults admit they're overwhelmed by information	75% of adults are looking for ways to live a more meaningful life	51% of people don't think it's important to attend church	46% of Americans say public schools are worse than 5 years ago	72% of women say they're stressed

#BarnaFrames

www.barnaframes.com

Barna Group

BEFORE YOU READ

....

- What is the very first image that comes to mind when you think of the word "violence"? Reflect on that image—why is it the first thing that came to your mind? Who are the faces that represent violence to you? Is there a present threat to you, or does the violence seem distant?

- How would you define the word "violence"?

- What does Jesus have to say about violence? What are some of his teachings that immediately come to mind when you think about his stance toward violence?

- In what ways do you think violent entertainment (TV, movies, video games, music) has affected you? Do you think it's made you more or less sensitive to real violence?

- War is a divisive topic for many people. What are your views on the morality of warfare—is there such a thing as a just war?

- When have you or someone you know experienced violence? How has that experience shaped you?

- Do you think we live in a "culture too comfortable with violence"? Why or why not?

FIGHTING FOR PEACE

Your Role in a Culture Too Comfortable with Violence

INFOGRAPHICS

I AM MOST CONCERNED ABOUT ...

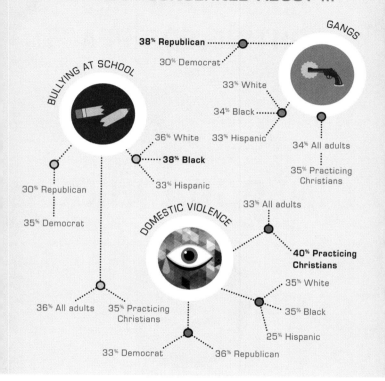

GANGS

BULLYING AT SCHOOL

38% Republican

30% Democrat

33% White

34% Black

36% White

33% Hispanic

38% Black

33% Hispanic

34% All adults

35% Practicing Christians

30% Republican

35% Democrat

33% All adults

DOMESTIC VIOLENCE

40% Practicing Christians

35% White

35% Black

36% All adults

35% Practicing Christians

25% Hispanic

33% Democrat

36% Republican

A growing UNEASE

While violence may seem like it's on the rise, so is people's discomfort about it. Nearly half of Americans say they've grown less comfortable with violence in the last decade. When asked what their top two concerns are when it comes to violence, adults identified the above.

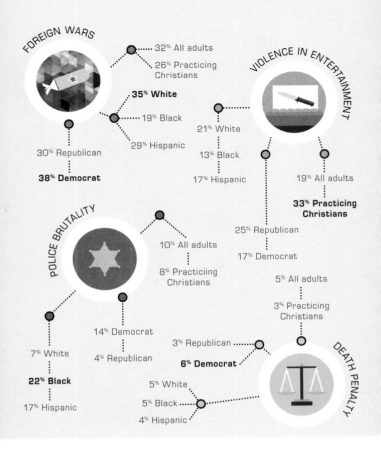

FOREIGN WARS
- 32% All adults
- 26% Practicing Christians
- **35% White**
- 19% Black
- 29% Hispanic
- 30% Republican
- **38% Democrat**

VIOLENCE IN ENTERTAINMENT
- 21% White
- 13% Black
- 17% Hispanic
- 19% All adults
- **33% Practicing Christians**
- 25% Republican
- 17% Democrat

POLICE BRUTALITY
- 10% All adults
- 8% Practiciing Christians
- 14% Democrat
- 4% Republican
- 7% White
- **22% Black**
- 17% Hispanic

DEATH PENALTY
- 5% All adults
- 3% Practicing Christians
- 3% Republican
- **6% Democrat**
- 5% White
- 5% Black
- 4% Hispanic

47% of adults say they've become less comfortable with violence over the last 10 years

Here we are now, ENTERTAIN US

Much ink has been spilled and studies done on the connections between violent entertainment and violent behavior. And, whether or not a true connection can be proven, adults certainly *perceive* that there is one. However, while Christians in particular are concerned about the effects of violence in entertainment, they are less likely to turn off a movie because of violence than most other offensive content.

33% Practicing Christians

and

19% All adults

rank the presence of violence in entertainment as one of their top two concerns when it comes to violence.

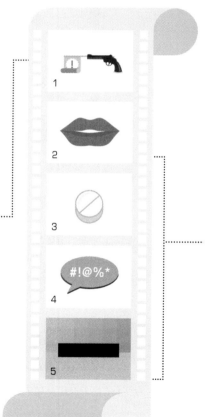

DO YOU THINK THERE IS A CONNECTION BETWEEN VIOLENT BEHAVIOR AND ...

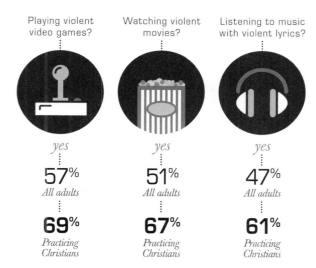

Playing violent video games?

yes

57%
All adults

69%
Practicing Christians

Watching violent movies?

yes

51%
All adults

67%
Practicing Christians

Listening to music with violent lyrics?

yes

47%
All adults

61%
Practicing Christians

WOULD YOU BE MORE LIKELY TO TURN OFF A MOVIE OR TV SHOW BECAUSE OF ...

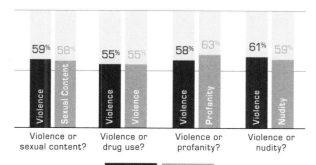

Violence or sexual content?	Violence or drug use?	Violence or profanity?	Violence or nudity?
Violence 59% / Sexual Content 58%	Violence 55% / Violence 55%	Violence 58% / Profanity 63%	Violence 61% / Nudity 59%

All adults Christians

FIGHTING FOR PEACE

Your Role in a Culture Too Comfortable with Violence

FRAMEWORK

BY BARNA GROUP

Violence is more pervasive than anyone cares to admit. You don't have to look hard to see the presence of violence in society today—from video games, television, and movies to war in far-off countries; from domestic violence to mass shootings in sleepy, upscale towns.

And because everyone has some sort of connection to the ugly topic of violence, arguments erupt over things like gun control, the effect of violent media on public attitudes and personal behaviors, the morality of drone strikes, and more.

The Relevance of Violence

The issues are complex and the answers far from simple; not surprisingly, Barna's FRAMES research revealed that many people struggle with this issue. We have produced this FRAME to provide insights on some of the most troubling aspects of violence, especially those that touch many of our lives:

Violent entertainment: The catalysts of popular culture—including music, television, movies, video gaming, and (often) sports—continue to mine violence for mindshare. Just think about the rise of blockbuster movies and television programs that literally need violence to progress their plots (e.g., movies like *Gladiator* and *Hunger Games*, television programs like *Breaking Bad* and *CSI,* games like *Call of Duty* and *World of Warcraft*). Violence has become big business. As residents of a global culture that is enraptured with violent entertainment, how can we fight for peace?

Video games: Today's youngest generations, including children, teens, and young adults, are particularly captivated by today's violent media, especially video games. If you are one of these teenagers or twentysomethings, how can you fight for peace when media make violence so easy to "play"?

Parents and violence: Among parents of this emerging generation, how can you fight for peace in this immersive media world of pixelated violence? And how can you send your children out into a world where violence threatens them in new and more intimate ways—from their schools to the movie theater?

The "just" use of force: Living in a free society is made possible by the rule of law and the appropriate use of violent force, whether by law enforcement or military. How can those who work in these arenas—police officers, soldiers, lawyers, judges, military chaplains, etc. —fight for peace?

Victims and doers of violence: Millions of people have been the victim of violence. Others have personally committed a violent act. Perhaps your experience with violence was private. Or maybe your community recently suffered a public display of violence. How can you fight for peace while being haunted by these acts?

Christians and violence: Finally, Christians represent an enormous part of the world's population—including a majority of the US population. As the globe's most powerful nation—one that is often more militaristic than we care to admit—what does it mean for Christ-followers in the United States to fight for peace—to support biblical policies and practices?

Violence in Numbers

The statistics related to violence are horrific: The number of homicides. The incidences of rape, domestic violence, battlefield casualties. But simply scrutinizing the numbers can mask the human side of humanity's impulse to harm others.

Our FRAMES research reveals nearly half of all adults today (47%) feel less comfortable with violence than they did 10 years ago. This increased discomfort is even more pronounced among women (55%), practicing Christians (59%), and the elderly (63%). However, the research also revealed one out of eight adults (12%) say they have become *more* comfortable with violence in recent years. This number is highest among Millennials—a full 20% of whom admit they are less sensitive to violence than they used to be. Despite the sheer volume of violence in entertainment as well as news reports about violent acts, a significant number of adults (42%) say their attitudes toward violence have not changed in the last ten years.

If violence is of increasing concern to most people, what tops their list of worries? About one-third of adults list bullying (36%), gangs (34%), domestic violence (33%), and foreign conflict (32%) as their top areas of concern. Among practicing Christians, two issues were more pronounced than among the general population: domestic violence and violence in entertainment.

With many sources putting the rate of domestic violence against women as high as one in four women, Christians have a good reason to be concerned.[1]

Undoubtedly, every church in America has within the congregation at least one woman suffering from some form of domestic abuse. However, as we'll see later on, the *ways* churches respond to victims of domestic violence who seek help is absolutely critical.

When it comes to violence in entertainment, Christians' views vary compared to all adults. The research shows Christians disapprove of violence in their entertainment. But given the choice, practicing Christians are more likely to turn off their movie or TV show if it features profanity, sexual content, or nudity than if it has violence. For non-Christians, such personal media choices reflect the opposite. They name violence as the top trigger for changing the channel, placing violence as more

Would you be more likely to turn off a movie or TV show because of ...

Violence or sexual content?

59%
All adults

58%
Practicing Christians

Violence or drug use?

55%
All adults

55%
Practicing Christians

Violence or profanity?

58%
All adults

63%
Practicing Christians

Violence or nudity?

61%
All adults

59%
Practicing Christians

objectionable than profanity, drug use, nudity, or sexual content.

Such differences relate to the question of whether violence on the screen leads to violence in real life. Though the academic literature on the subject is divided, the public perception is that there is a connection between consumption of violent media and perpetrating violent acts. Notably, adults believe the type of media consumed affects the stickiness of the violence: 47% believe music with violent lyrics leads to aggressive behavior, growing to 51% who believe the same for movies, and 57% who connect playing violent video games to real-world brutality.

Evangelical Christians are significantly more likely (80% compared to 57% of all adults) to say violent video games are connected to violent actions. They are also more likely (74% compared to 51% of all adults) to say violent movies lead to violence.

Millennials (18- to 29-year-olds in this study) are more accepting of violence compared to other generations. Nearly half of young adults (48%) feel that "none" of the media are connected to violent behavior. The older the adult, the more likely they are to be concerned that media links to aggressive behavior. Are younger adults more conditioned to be comfortable with violence? Do they view media in a different way than other adults and are thus less prone to judge their effects?

Justifying Violence

If most people are concerned with a culture of violence, where they disagree is in terms of how to stop it. One area of strong controversy is guns. Four in ten Americans say they are against any law that gets in the way of gun ownership while nearly the same number (37%) express a desire for more restrictions on gun ownership. Just under half of Americans (46%) believe that those gun ownership restrictions would ultimately lead to less gun violence. Of course, that leaves half who would disagree—accounting for the continued and deep divide over this issue. The opinions run along political lines: Democrats are the strongest supporters of more gun laws—two-thirds of whom say more restrictions on gun ownership would lead to less gun violence, while Republicans are the least likely to agree with that statement (20%). Women (50%) and blacks (55%) are also much more likely to be in favor of gun restrictions, while men (41%) and practicing Christians (40%) remain more skeptical.

On one violent concept, however, most Americans can agree. Nearly two-thirds of Americans (60%) say they have the right to defend themselves, even if it requires violence to do so.

Americans, in general, are less sure about foreign wars and political forms of violence. Less than half of Americans would say violence is appropriate in the defense of freedom (44%) and only about one-quarter (27%) believe they have a patriotic duty to support war. Support for nuclear weapons is even lower, with less

Americans
AND THEIR GUNS

Want to start an argument among friends? Bring up gun ownership.
It's a topic that deeply divides Americans—and Christians.

40%
ALL ADULTS
"I'm against any law that gets in the way of law-abiding citizens owning guns"

37%
ALL ADULTS
"I think there should be more restrictions on gun ownership in the US"

"If there were more restrictions on gun ownership, there would be less gun violence"

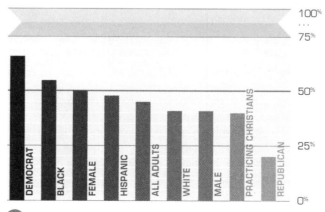

than one in four Americans saying nuclear weapons are necessary.

Would Jesus Really Turn the Other Cheek?

Jesus' recorded words include "Blessed are the peacemakers" and "Pray for your enemies." The FRAMES research reveals that people (Christians included) are much more likely to support violence than they believe Jesus would. In other words, they believe one thing about violence even though they believe Jesus' stance is different.

The data reveal the average adult in the United States perceives Jesus as a peacemaker at heart. Very few adults surmise that Jesus would support violence in retribution for family attack (5%), public execution of criminals (5%), or stockpiling nuclear weapons as a deterrent against foreign attack (2%). Instead, more than one-third (37%) believe Jesus would want more people against war in general.

The same is true when it comes to less institutional and more personal motives for violence. While three in five Americans (and a nearly equal number of practicing Christians, 57%) would say they have a right to defend themselves with violence, only one in ten (11%) think Jesus would agree with them.

These are just some of the many striking inconsistencies in American perceptions of violence, and the tenuous relationship between the Christian faith and understanding violence and peace.

Rebuilding a theology and practice of peace will take more than just engaging the gun reform debate or changing the channel from violent images — though it might include these things.

We know we can't answer all the questions when it comes to violence, but we believe we can shed light on some practical ways to live as peacemakers in a culture too comfortable with violence. In this FRAME, we join Carol Howard Merritt, a Presbyterian pastor and author who has worked in a number of urban and inner-city neighborhoods and who interacts regularly with both perpetrators and victims of violence, and Tyler Wigg-Stevenson, a pastor and founder of the Two Futures Project, a group working toward the abolition of nuclear weapons. Both bring considerable personal experience and biblical wisdom to this complicated issue shaping our world. ◆

FIGHTING FOR PEACE

Your Role in a Culture Too Comfortable with Violence

THE FRAME

BY TYLER WIGG-STEVENSON

I've been a peace activist for nearly fifteen years, but nothing has brought the shadow of violence home to me like becoming a soon-to-be father, who often finds himself literally sleepless with excitement about meeting his daughter.

By the time these words become ink on a page, we'll have welcomed our littlest love, God willing— a tiny, needy, desperately vulnerable body with a disproportionately loud voice, whose mere arrival makes the world seem orders of magnitude more terrifying than it did nine months ago. I don't know how our poll respondents decided which kinds of violence scare them the most. The prospect of raising a young girl certainly makes the threats of bullying and domestic violence loom larger than they did before. But war, gangs, the death penalty, police brutality, and nuclear weapons— they've all got me worried.

I've even started to ask myself questions that would have struck my teenage self as decidedly stuffy, like: When do we turn off the TV? What will we say when she wants to see her first R-rated movie? What (and when) is too much? How will we know?

We live in a profoundly violent culture. I know it, and you know it. That's why you've bothered to pick up this FRAME. It's the strangest thing, because even though we know it and even though we sense it, most of the time violence still seems so distant. Wars are fought far away. We feel safe in our homes, on our streets.

Some of us do, at least. Not every reader will have this

perception. For some, the culture of violence is all too near: an unsafe relationship, a troubled neighborhood, an encounter with law enforcement, perhaps even *being* law enforcement. Others may have the experience of being the victim of violent crime or being the perpetrator. Still others worry for a child, parent, or sibling in uniform somewhere where people shoot at them.

Maybe it's just that we can remember a time when reports of mass shootings still surprised us—when we couldn't recite their now-familiar formula: young male shooter, history of mental illness, dead on the scene, hundreds of rounds of ammunition, dozens of casualties. Our thoughts and prayers are with the victims. Wait three months. Repeat.

WHAT IS VIOLENCE?

So, for whatever reason, we've got this hunch. We know we live in a violent culture. It's why nearly half of all adults—and 60% of practicing Christians—surveyed for our FRAMES research say they've become less comfortable with violence over the last decade.

Violence is a tricky topic, though. I thought I knew exactly what I thought about it until I started to think about it. On one level it's pretty straightforward: Violence is *force that hurts, damages.*

However, the more I pondered, the more complicated it got.

After all, some sorts of violence we all agree on. Nobody thinks bullying is good, or gang violence, or murder. We disagree only on how big a deal they are and what should be done about them.

Other forms of violence are more controversial. The death penalty is violent, but is it wrong? Should it be used only in certain circumstances? How about the police using lethal force? When is it okay? When isn't it? What about self-defense? What about defending your family?

Then there's war. Is it ever justifiable? Does it depend on which war? World War II, Vietnam, Afghanistan—are those different? Why? Are nuclear weapons a necessary evil? Are they evil at all? Can Christians ever think any evil is necessary?

These are questions without easy answers. Unsurprisingly, our FRAMES research shows such questions (and the ways we answer them) deeply divide Americans—and Christians.

The trouble with focusing on these questions is they let most of us off the hook. After all, I'm not a violent man, right? Sure, I like football, and I've done a bit of boxing. But other things—war and gang violence and terrorism? Yes, they scare me, but I'm not going to *do* them.

So, a violent culture is something that happens *to* me and mine. It's not something I help create.

Right?

OWNING THE PROBLEM

Here's the problem I can't escape: Our culture wouldn't be so violent if we didn't like violence so much.

And that includes me.

This is absolutely essential to realize if we're going to take spiritual responsibility for our situation. If I think about violence as something *other people* do, then I can get away with thinking the solution is to solve their behavior. But that would be to ignore what is the heart of the matter: why my own heart cherishes violence.

That's what we're going to think about here. As a theologian, pastor, husband, and father, I want to know why I like violence. What does liking violence do to me? What does a culture of violence mean for me, as someone who tries to follow the Prince of Peace?

Why Do We Like Violence?

Not everyone likes violence, I suppose, but enough of us do so that it's become good business to produce violent films and television, make violent video games, and write violent books. How much money do we spend to see people get hurt in thousands of different ways? Does anyone know? Billions, certainly.

Violence is a weird thing to enjoy. Violence is different, after all, than our other extreme impulses. Fat and sugar taste delicious; that's why we eat too much of them. Sex feels fantastic, primally so; that's why we crave it. But violence? Violence *hurts*. So, why on earth do we want it so badly?

Why is it that if I get an email with a link to the "Monster Hits" video compilation from Sunday's games, I'm clicking it? Why did I laugh until I cried when I saw the slapstick tricks—in retrospect, so brutal!—inflicted by Kevin McCallister upon Joe Pesci's and Daniel Stern's "Wet Bandits" in *Home Alone*? Why do I long to see the bad guy get what he deserves at the end of an action film—to be righteously blasted, or sucked into a jet engine, or whatever?

I'm not saying these reactions are positive, sanctified—but they are real and perfectly average. Many generally decent human beings evidently like seeing people hurt—at least when they know it's pretend.

I can't speak to the psychological reasons, but I've got a theological theory: We like violence because *it feeds the part of us that wants to live in a world without God.*

Violence does this by telling us two lies, two myths, about the world. The first myth of violence is basic atheism: *There is no God*, so we can't be made in the divine image like Genesis says we are. That means our bodies are just meat, without spirit, to do with as we please.

The second myth of violence is more insidious: *God without a cross*, or the "myth of redemptive violence." It says good wins out by killing the bad guys—instead of

by dying for them. It is the dead opposite of the gospel
of Jesus.

When we're entertained by violence, we're believing the
lie told by one or both of these myths. They let us enjoy
something that shouldn't be enjoyable.

We are defined by what we love. That's why heart-work
is the core of the Christian life, as defined by the two
great commandments to love God and love neighbor.
When violence entertains us, we're loving *wrong*. We're
loving and delighting in a world without God and/or a
world without the gospel.

THE FIRST MYTH OF VIOLENCE:
A WORLD WITHOUT GOD

I was just old enough to watch R-rated movies when
Mel Gibson's *Braveheart* hit the big screen in 1995,
and I loved it as much as every other 18-year-old boy
did. Mostly I remember That Scene with the Mace,
which graphically showed one soldier braining another.
The scene was deeply controversial, with many critics
asking whether we had crossed a line in our depictions
of violence (today that line has disappeared past the
horizon in our rearview mirror). The group of teenage
boys I saw the movie with responded — not atypically,
I imagine — with semi-horrified glee.

What was going on there? Why did we react this way
to seeing people cut down?

The essential element of this kind of violence is that it happens to *characters* — to bodies — without histories or context. In other words, it's violence done to people who aren't really people. The sheer body count in any modern action flick depends on this illusion. The English soldiers readily dispatched by William Wallace's troops in *Braveheart* are — in fact, must be — men without wives, mothers, siblings, children, friends. They are props.

Let's consider what would happen if we shattered this fantasy. Imagine if, at the moment before a heroic Scotsman's mace pulped an English skull like a cantaloupe, the main plot stopped and went back in time to patiently tell the story of the doomed man: his birth, boyhood, and relationship with his parents; his first kiss, first love, eventual marriage to a Yorkshire girl, and birth of his own children; his training as a tradesman and the circumstances of his eventual conscription in the English king's army; his terror on the morning of battle and that awful, final charge.

If the film did all this before bringing us back to the moment when his head and face are unceremoniously destroyed by someone demonstrating all the care of a man cutting grass, none of us would respond with a thrilled grunt.

Because real people are not disposable.

When we thrill to see bodies turned into so much cannon fodder, we're buying into the story that humans don't really matter at all.

In the thematic climax to *Catch-22*, Joseph Heller's classic black comedy about World War II, the protagonist, Yossarian, sits next to his dying, eviscerated friend, Snowden.

> It was easy to read the message in his entrails. Man was matter, that was Snowden's secret. Drop him out a window and he'll fall. Set fire to him and he'll burn. Bury him and he'll rot, like other kinds of garbage. The spirit gone, man is garbage. That was Snowden's secret. Ripeness was all.[2]

This is our choice: a spirit-filled body or garbage. If our viewing habits are any indicator, our culture is obsessed with stories about the latter. Such stories let us believe we can do whatever we want with bodies: That they are just there for our entertainment and that what we do physically has no consequences for our souls.

The point isn't that we live this way all the time. I don't think I'm just meat, of course, nor are my loved ones. But this myth bleeds into real life every time we treat others' bodies, or our own, simply as matter to be used in whatever way we please. In this respect, at least, there is no difference between the proliferation of violent entertainment and pornography — the latter is the former and vice versa. They're both stories where human bodies aren't sacred, made in God's image, but are just meat to be butchered and holes to be filled.

THE SECOND MYTH OF VIOLENCE: GOD WITHOUT A CROSS

You don't need to see most action movies to summarize them. Most of us can recite the basic script from memory: A good guy is pushed to the brink by bad guys and has to go beyond the rules of "polite society" to keep the rest of us safe. It's the premise of genre mainstays like *Die Hard* and the *Bourne* movies along with thousands of lesser-known titles.

It's also the explicit ethos of US Marine Col. Nathan Jessup, Jack Nicholson's ruthless character in the classic *A Few Good Men*. Facing off with Tom Cruise's Lt. Daniel Kaffee, Jessup proclaims:

> Son, we live in a world that has walls, and those walls have to be guarded by men with guns. Who's gonna do it? You?... My existence, while grotesque and incomprehensible to you, saves lives. You don't want the truth because deep down in places you don't talk about at parties, you want me on that wall—you *need* me on that wall.[3]

Though Jessup is the film's antihero, his self-defense in the courtroom makes many viewers nod approvingly. Isn't this our world, after all? At the end of the day, the only way to live is to threaten violent domination.

Moreover, this isn't just a theme in film, books, and video games—it goes to the heart of how we justify actions like the practice of torture for intelligence gathering, or the existence of CIA "Black Site" prisons, which operated outside the reach of the law. It's a view that evidently makes sense to Christians and nonbelievers alike.

The late theologian and biblical scholar Walter Wink coined the term "the myth of redemptive violence" to describe this belief that violence saves: It is "the victory of order over chaos by means of violence," the idea that violence is simply "what works."[4] The insight came to him while thinking about the perpetual conflict between Bluto and Popeye in the cartoon:

> The format never varies. Neither party ever gains any insight or learns from these encounters. They never sit down and discuss their differences. Repeated defeats do not teach Bluto to honour Olive Oyl's humanity, and repeated pummelings do not teach Popeye to swallow his spinach before the fight.[5]

What most of us don't realize is how fundamentally pagan this attitude toward violence is. Wink traces it back to the *Enuma elis*, an ancient Babylonian creation story. According to the *Enuma elis*, history gets going when the youngest god, Marduk, kills his mother, Tiamat, splits her open, and makes the world out of her corpse. Unlike the biblical creation story of a good God creating a good world, in the Babylonian account, "evil is simply a primordial fact."[6]

As a result, violence continues in an endless cycle. In today's stories, Wink argues, "only the names have changed" — our children may not learn about Marduk, but "from the earliest age, children are awash in depictions of violence as the ultimate solution to human conflicts."[7]

EYE FOR AN EYE

Should be the primary philosophy of punishment in our society

19%

All adults

12%

Practicing Christians

TURN THE OTHER CHEEK

Should be the primary philosophy of punishment in our society

5%

All adults

7%

Practicing Christians

Let us be totally clear: The myth of redemptive violence is the satanic inversion of the Christian gospel. It is finally and completely incompatible with Jesus Christ crucified. If the myth of redemptive violence were the Good News of Jesus Christ, then the messiah would have killed his enemies instead of dying for them (as imagined in the 2013 *Saturday Night Live* digital short, "DJesus Uncrossed"[8]). If the myth were true, then we would all be dead, because by nature we are enemies of God (see Romans 5:10).

Instead, the Good News of Jesus Christ is that God has come in the flesh to endure violence on our behalf and in our place—not to inflict it. (Keep reading to see how this relates to the violence of the second coming and the final judgment.)

Unfortunately, as Wink

notes, no "religious system has even remotely rivaled the myth of redemptive violence in its ability to catechise its young so totally."[9] Redemptive violence just makes sense in a fallen world. Good guys need to beat the bad guys. Outside the cross of Jesus Christ—and those who have lived by its power—human history lacks compelling evidence that it's better to be weak than strong. A "god" who destroys evil is much safer, more understandable, and more intuitive than one who can forgive murderers, love rapists, and call me equally a sinner, though I have never done such deeds.

NAMING THE PERVERSION

In our FRAMES research, practicing Christians were much more likely to believe there is a connection between violent behavior and the consumption of violent media, though the data correlating the two is notoriously inconclusive.[10]

As Christians, however, we know outward actions aren't the only barometer of our well-being. It's not enough to refrain from bad deeds; the state of our hearts matters as well (see Matthew 5:21–30). This means we fight a continual battle for the state of our souls. The words of video game critic Erik Kain are thus less than comforting:

> The vast majority of people who play [games like *Grand Theft Auto V*]—hopefully the adults who play it, and not impressionable children—see this experience as one of virtual, temporary, and entirely fantastical debauchery.... Most people can see this for what it is: escapism.[11]

I believe there is a connection between violent behavior and …

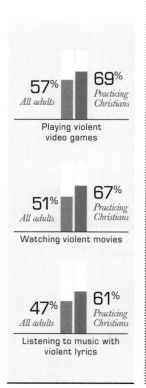

57%
All adults

69%
Practicing Christians

Playing violent
video games

51%
All adults

67%
Practicing Christians

Watching violent movies

47%
All adults

61%
Practicing Christians

Listening to music with
violent lyrics

Yes, precisely. When we are entertained by violence, we "escape" into a world where one (or both) of the myths about violence is true. Just because this doesn't turn us into serial killers doesn't make it all right. These forms of escapism put a tension in our hearts. They preserve the parts of us that long for the myths of a world without God or a world without the cross.

This addiction is nothing new. But we perhaps forget, as other eras did not, the powerful draw and genuine spiritual damage of being violently entertained.

In St. Augustine's *Confessions*, he describes his friend Alypius being dragged by friends against his will to the gladiatorial games, which Alypius opposed on moral grounds. Alypius sat with eyes firmly shut, determined to remain above the fray, but:

Would that he had shut his ears also! For when one of the combatants fell in the fight, a mighty cry from the whole audience stirred him so strongly that, overcome by curiosity and still prepared (as he thought) to despise and rise superior to it no matter what it was, he opened his eyes and *was struck with a deeper wound in his soul than the victim whom he desired to see had been in his body*. Thus he fell more miserably than the one whose fall had raised that mighty clamor which had entered through his ears and unlocked his eyes to make way for the wounding and beating down of his soul.... For, as soon as he saw the blood, he drank in with it a savage temper, and he did not turn away, but fixed his eyes on the bloody pastime, unwittingly drinking in the madness.... He was now no longer the same man who came in, but was one of the mob he came into, a true companion of those who had brought him thither.[12]

Now, we should celebrate that we live in an age when public death is no longer considered entertainment. Whatever you think of capital punishment, it's a good thing it's no longer a spectacle; it's good that gladiator death matches have been replaced by football rivalries and that lethal chariot races have been replaced by NASCAR. The real dangers of our current sports don't make them morally equivalent to the vicious games of the past. Our sensibilities have changed.

But not our hearts. This means we're every bit as vulnerable as Alypius, whose reaction to the arena violence is described by Augustine as akin to spiritual murder. Every addict is just one step away from relapse.

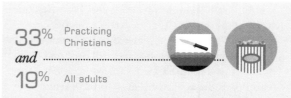

33% Practicing Christians

and

19% All adults

rank its presence in entertainment as one of their top two concerns when it comes to violence

When we allow our hearts to be shaped in ways that delight in violence — even if it is make-believe — we resist being formed ever more completely to the image of Jesus.

KICKING THE HABIT

If we're going to follow Jesus in a culture of violence, we have to find a way to hate violence, rather than be entertained by it. To kick the habit of violence, we have to experience violence for what it is.

That is, we have to let violence hurt.

I recently heard a lecture about the first genocide of the twentieth century in which Turkish forces killed perhaps one million Armenians. One of the sepia-toned slides showed the half-naked corpse of what looked to be a teenager who was so emaciated that you couldn't tell whether it was a boy or girl. The body lay on its back with the knees bent and slightly splayed—a pose totally devoid of dignity. I stared at the slide for a moment, and then I had to turn away. Looking at the picture felt like holding my hand to a hot stove.

We've all been there. The initial sight of violence—a car accident, a photo from a faraway war—captivates our attention, draws our eyes, but we can't look too long. When violence isn't wrapped in an entertaining package, it's actually painful to see or hear about.

Why? Of course it makes sense that it hurts to be on the receiving end of violence. That's what violence does: It hurts. But violence doesn't hurt only the person it's directed against. It can hurt the people who see it and—as the leaders of the Civil Rights Movement knew—violence hurts the people who do it, even if they don't know it.

What's going on inside us when we hurt seeing violence?

It's a matter of empathy. The word comes from the Greek *empatheia*, literally meaning "in-feeling": to experience empathy is to be *in* the feelings of someone else. Empathy is a deeper and far more vulnerable emotion than sympathy. Empathy means "with-feeling." It's one thing to feel sorry *for* someone. It's another to experience their pain as your own.

Almost everybody feels empathy with certain people—our families and closest friends. But Christians fighting for peace in a violent culture can't stop at what we might call "natural" empathy.

Instead, we need to be training our souls to feel a holier kind of love—an empathy like Jesus'—encompassing friend and enemy alike. "If you love those who love you ... what are you doing more than others? Do not even pagans do that?" (Matthew 5:46–47) Instead, Jesus' followers are to "be perfect ... as your heavenly Father is perfect" (Matthew 5:48). Here, the "perfection" of God refers to the fact that his love doesn't discriminate. This kind of empathy comes from recognizing that every person is made in the image of God (see Genesis 1:26–27).

If we're going to let violence hurt, we have to push past the limits of our natural empathy. These limits hit home for me while watching the breakout HBO hit *Game of Thrones*—an epic drama known for its massive cast of well-developed characters, as well as its copious depictions of violence and sex. Caught up by the gripping, sprawling tale, I'd rationalized my way through it.

The season three finale undid me, though, with a scene of graphic brutality against a pregnant woman: Multiple men stabbed her repeatedly in the stomach before leaving her to die in despair, clutching her bloody belly. It is an image that is painful even to type; I found it catastrophic to watch, but I was so shocked I couldn't turn away in time to avoid the sight. Since then, the scene has taken up residence like a parasite in my memory, cropping up without warning or welcome.

Here's the problem: The dozens of hours of *Game of Thrones* that preceded this one had also been filled with brutalized bodies. What was different here? Only this: My wife, pregnant with our unborn child, slept in the next room. Every day since she'd begun to show, Natalie and I had marveled at her growing tummy with delight and wonder. Her belly seemed to have its own personality. We treated it with all the infinite tenderness we wanted to impart to the small person growing inside. So, when I saw that character's pregnant body desecrated, it wasn't just something "out there." It hit home.

To my great shame, my reaction to this one scene made me realize I had watched countless bodies violated in other episodes without any similar pangs. Violence only seemed to bother me when the people who suffered looked like my loved ones. Evidently I had little problem with death and dismemberment in general.

FROM NATURAL EMPATHY TO HOLY LOVE

Indiscriminate love doesn't come naturally—if it did, we wouldn't need Jesus. Instead, we have to train ourselves to feel it.

My dad has inspired me in this regard. After a long and successful career as a computer programmer, he could have retired to the golf course. Instead, he now spends much of his time down at the local prison, teaching peaceful conflict resolution to incarcerated men through a program called the Alternatives to Violence Project (AVP).[13] A big part of the AVP curriculum is learning how to put yourself in the other guy's shoes. It's not easy, in or out of prison. Developing empathy that goes beyond our nearest and dearest takes work, and, just like physical fitness, the price we pay for this strength of heart is suffering.

In his book *Righteous Gentiles of the Holocaust*, the ethicist David Gushee asked what led a small number of Gentiles to risk their lives to save Jews from the Nazis, while the vast majority of non-Jews, almost all of them "Christian," did nothing. His findings, based on first-hand accounts and historical records, should unsettle anyone who feels comfortable in their faith. The vast majority of Europeans were Christians, after all—but Gushee found that the tiny percentage of people who put their own lives on the line for strangers didn't do so because they were "super-Christians" or experts in doctrine.[14]

No. The common denominator was whether they had experienced suffering themselves. Whether they were devoutly pious or essentially irreligious, those who had suffered were more willing to save these suffering strangers. That is, their own experience of pain had expanded their empathy past its "natural" limits. They didn't see what Hitler's propagandists wanted them to see: the hated, sub-human "Jew." They just saw human beings like themselves.

Don't get me wrong: I'm not endorsing suffering for suffering's sake. The church has a terrible history of blessing the hardship of oppressed people as a spiritual good—from slavery to domestic abuse—when it should have instead decried the injustice and rushed to serve its victims. Moreover, suffering can also make people numb and hard-hearted.

In a world where violence is everywhere, though, we've got three options for how we deal with it.

1 We can enjoy it, maybe even perpetrate it, letting it feed the myths of a world without God and a God without a cross and cultivating hard-heartedness at the suffering of others.

2 We can turn away from it, trying to carve out a censored, perfectly safe life — ignoring the violence done on our behalf, or the subtle ways we're complicit in it.

Or,

3 We can let our hearts be broken, over and over again, wherever we find the world breaking people.

Option 3 answers the practical question of whether it's ever okay to watch, view, or read depictions of violence. The short answer, in my view, is "yes," as long as we see it for exactly what it is, which is the degradation of human beings made in God's image.

Georges Bataille, a controversial twentieth century French philosopher, writes about his reaction to a photograph of a young Chinese man who had been tortured to death in the Boxer Rebellion:

> I loved him with a love in which the sadistic instinct played no part: he communicated his pain to me or

perhaps the excessive nature of his pain, and it was precisely that which I was seeking, not so as to take pleasure in it, but in order to ruin in me that which is opposed to ruin.[15]

Bataille was no Christian, but here he grasps a fundamental truth of Jesus. Violence hurts. Period. When we experience it for what it is, instead of the entertaining packages we usually wrap it in, we don't build up our tolerance for it. Quite the opposite: We build up our vulnerability to it. This can happen whether the depiction is real or fictional. The question we need to ask ourselves is what does the violence do to us?

Does it titillate, entertain, and inflame us — as the gladiator arena did to Alypius, and as unrepentant "torture porn" like the *Saw* film franchise does today?

Or does it do something else? Does it show the humanity beneath the suffering? Does it serve as a cautionary tale? Does it reveal the true horror of violence as experienced by so many through war, abuse, bullying, and so on? Does it arouse our compassion? Does it draw us deeper into the blessed condition of mourning for the world as it presently is (see Matthew 5:4)?

The closer our experience of violence is to the one who suffers it — that is, the more universal and unrestricted our empathy — the closer we are to the mind of Christ.

Earlier this year I led a group of Christians on a trip to Japan. We had the privilege to see some film footage taken by US Army personnel in Nagasaki immediately after the atomic bombing. It showed a teenage boy being treated for burns that took the skin from his back, buttocks, and legs. As the camera stays steady, he lies facedown, unable to move, while hands swab and anoint the sheets of writhing, red, raw muscle. He lay in this position for two years; we watched for perhaps sixty seconds. It wasn't entertaining.

We didn't know this boy. He didn't command our natural empathy, but we couldn't see him as anything less than the image of God. We saw how violence had tried to render him into so much wreck, a slab of butcher's work. We didn't turn away.

The image of God, ruined by violence?

Look up. We have arrived at the foot of the cross.

THE VIOLENCE OF GOD

Christians cannot confront the problem of violence without wrestling with the violence of God. It's obvious to anyone who reads the Bible: It's a violent book. People often talk about the "Old Testament God" and the "New Testament God" as if these were two different divinities, but that's nonsense. The OT has its holy wars and slaughter, but its body count and horror pales before the violence of Revelation. There is one God in the Bible; he brings prosperity and creates disaster (see Isaiah 45:7).

Our God is a violent God.

As Andy Crouch recently observed, however, God's creativity is more fundamental than God's violence—on either side of the violence of history, there's the awesome beauty of creation and the spectacular beauty of the new creation (compare Genesis 1–2 and Revelation 21–22).[16]

Seeing this ultimate creative purpose helps us grasp the nature of divine violence. It is a holy God's response to a world gone terribly wrong through its own sin and wickedness. That is, God's violence is righteous judgment. In the biblical history, that judgment disciplines wrongdoing. The violence recorded in Revelation—the apocalypse—is part of the final judgment before all things are made new.

The judgment of God allows us to understand the connection between human violence and justice. Because of sin, our world is unavoidably violent. Rather than embracing that fact, Christians will always strive to place our violence under the discipline of justice. This subordination of violence to justice goes to the heart of at least one biblically grounded political theology, which sees a justice-disciplined power serving as a proxy for the judgment of God (see Romans 13:1–7). God's judgment actually withholds us from the full potential of our sinfulness (see, for example, the *katechon*, or "withholder," in 2 Thessalonians 2:6–7).

This is why most denominations allow Christians to serve in certain professions that involve violence, like the military, police, or as judges. The force they wield is supposed to be used to serve the purpose of justice and restrain wickedness. For many, this type of violence is viewed as coherent with a biblical faith. Other Christian traditions, such as the Anabaptists, have rejected involvement in these professions as irreconcilable with the commandments of the Lord. But the violence inherent in these callings makes them spiritually dangerous, as well, because it puts people in situations of violence most of us will never face.

The early church recognized the tension between discipleship and violence: It prohibited judges or military commanders from joining the church unless they quit their jobs, because their duties included executions, which the early church believed a faith in Jesus prohibited.[17] Disciples of Jesus in similar occupations today must have a double dose of spiritual discipline to ensure they do not abuse the power they are to wield on behalf of justice. Congregations that count military or law enforcement among their members owe them a special level of spiritual care as these members wrestle with specialized problems of conscience and moral injury.[18]

The most important example of divine violence, however, is not at the front or back of the biblical narrative. It's at the middle, where God doesn't inflict violence—he suffers it.

THE VIOLENCE OF THE CROSS

For me, the most unsettling section of the FRAMES data was the difference between practicing Christians' attitudes to violence and what they thought Jesus would think. In question after question — from self-defense and gun ownership to the death penalty and nuclear weapons — Christians said one thing while admitting they thought Jesus would answer differently. Six in ten adults — and nearly the same number of practicing Christians (57%) — for example, say they have the right to defend themselves, even if it requires violence. Yet only one in ten adults (11%) believe Jesus would agree. Nearly half of Christians (46%) and four in ten Americans are against gun restrictions, but only 7% of adults think Jesus would be. When it comes to the death penalty, about four in ten Americans (and Christians) support it, but only 5% think Jesus would. About a quarter of Americans — Christian or otherwise — believe nuclear weapons are necessary to keep our enemies from attacking us. Only 2% of Americans think Jesus would agree.

In summary, Christian opinions about violence look more like those of nonbelievers than what they think are the views of Jesus.

This leads to a disturbing conclusion: Our violence problem is a belief problem. It means we haven't really understood the cross of Christ because the cross teaches us everything we need to know about violence. There we see all the most fundamental questions of a violent culture — and how the Son of God responds to it. The cross isn't just the place where Jesus happened to die. No: The crucifixion is God's self-portrait.

First, the cross teaches us that the most fundamental question about violence isn't whether it's legitimate, but it brings up the question of God's relationship to

What would
JESUS THINK?

There's a big difference between what people personally
believe when it comes to violence and what they
think Jesus would believe—even among Christians.

"I have the right to defend
myself, even if it requires
violence"

60%
57%
11%

"Nuclear weapons are
absolutely necessary to keep
our enemies from attacking us"

23%
24%
2%

"If someone does violence
to my family, I have a right
to do the same to them"

21%
11%
5%

"Acts of violence are
sometimes necessary
to defend freedom"

44%
47%
10%

"The government should
have the option to execute
the worst criminals"

38%
40%
5%

"I'm against any law that gets
in the way of law-abiding
citizens owning guns"

40%
46%
7%

"I have a patriotic duty
to support the wars
my country fights"

26%
25%
7%

"I think there should be more
restrictions on gun ownership
in the US"

37%
34%
21%

■ All adults   ■ Practicing Christians   ■ What would Jesus think?

violence itself. After all, if we ask questions about what kinds of violence are legitimate and what kinds aren't, which was the cross? On the one hand it was utterly illegitimate—a travesty of legal procedure, the lynching of the world's only truly innocent man, the murder of the Son of God. On the other, it could not have happened if God had not allowed it (see John 19:11).

Second, the cross shows us the myths that let us enjoy violence. Spectators walked past the cross and laughed, entertained by the show. They took it as evidence that the God of Jesus was nowhere to be found. They despised and scorned the notion that any true Messiah would rather die than kill (see Matthew 27:38–44).

The Jesuit theologian Jon Sobrino writes: "Rather than viewing the cross as some arbitrary design on God's part, we must see it as the outcome of God's primordial option: the incarnation. The cross is the outcome of an incarnation"—that is, God becoming human in Jesus Christ—"situated in a world of sin that is revealed to be a power working against the God of Jesus."[19] That's why the cross shows us—more than God's violent judgment in history, more than the holy wars of Israel, more than the terrors of the apocalypse—what it means to draw close to the heart of God in the midst of a violent culture.

The cross reveals the cycle of violence can be broken when we refuse to return evil for evil and forgive those who do harm.

The cross means God's justice will prevail over all of our

violence — that beyond all violence lies the possibility of creation.

The cross means the hope of life is greater than the power to inflict death.

But the cross means these things *only* when we receive it in faith — when we look to the cross and exclaim, with the centurion, "Surely this man was the Son of God!" (Mark 15:39).

Many will not do this. They will look at the cross and see proof that violence wins. They will see it as the sacrificial altar of an absent God. They will be delighted and titillated to see proof our bodies are just garbage.

It is up to us to decide not to laugh or be entertained. It is up to us to see the spirit *in* the blood and bile. It is up to us to see the Son of God who takes the place of every defiled body, and who stands with every body that continues to be violated today. It is up to us to take our stand there. With them. With him.

We can do this because his broken body and shed blood — the result of violence — have been given to us, for us. In that divine ruin we find the mystery of restoration. ◆

FIGHTING FOR PEACE

Your Role in a Culture Too Comfortable with Violence

THE FRAME

BY CAROL HOWARD MERRITT

Like a keening chorus of mourning, my Twitter feed erupted into 140-character prayers from across the country.

"Lord, have mercy on Sandy Hook."

"Our prayers are with the parents in Newtown."

"Oh God, why? #sandyhook"

"What happened?" I thought. "What's Sandy Hook?" I typed a news site's Web address into my browser. Oversized headlines screamed the devastating events continuing to unfold in Newtown, Connecticut. I soon learned Sandy Hook was an elementary school in Newtown where Adam Lanza, a twenty-year-old gunman, had killed his mother, twenty children, six adults, and himself. I scrolled down the page to see photos of tiny children, faces stricken by shock and terror, moving hand in hand to a safe place outside the school building. Another photo showed a woman hunched over, clutching her chest and crying into her cell phone, her features contorted by fear and grief.

I stared at the image of the young white man who had fired so many fatal shots, and his wide eyes stared back with vacant indifference. Lanza's neck barely filled his collar, his pale face gaunt and drawn. Seeing his wide-eyed countenance, my own prayers swelled up with the others, "Lord, have mercy."

It felt all too familiar.

Only a few months earlier, I had sat next to my daughter in a movie, scanning the darkened theater with

real fear. It was the day after James Eagan Holmes had
entered a similar theater during a midnight screening
of *The Dark Knight Rises*. He stood at the front of the
theater with his hair dyed orange-red, and the audience
couldn't delineate entertainment from devastation —
no one moved, no one got up. He filled the crowded
theater with smoke and began shooting, killing twelve
people and injuring seventy others.

And then there was that same chorus of shocked tweets
when the news broke that seventeen-year-old Trayvon
Martin, an unarmed African-American high school
student, had been shot by a man who was part of
a neighborhood watch program in Sanford, Florida.
George Zimmerman, a multi-racial Hispanic man,
claimed self-defense, as the two had fought first. His
claim held up in court, backed by Florida's stand-
your-ground law. Another Twitter frenzy — this time
a divisive debate over gun laws and racial equity.

In Boston, celebrations after the marathon were
interrupted by explosions. In Nairobi, bombs ripped
through a shopping mall. So many dead. So many
wounded.

All this within the span of twelve months — tragedies
bombarding us from all sides. And it does not stop with
gun violence or terrorist attacks. The past two years
have seen an epidemic of teens committing suicide after
intense bullying by classmates at school and online. In
some cases, physical assault and threats accompanied
verbal harassment, but in others, the unrelenting
violence of words just became too much to bear.
For too many young men and women, one last act

of self-inflicted violence is preferable to the constant cruelty inflicted by their peers.

Instances of violence in other countries confront us in the daily headlines as well. In the fall of 2013, the Syrian regime used weaponized nerve gas to kill more than 1,400 civilians—including more than 400 children—in an area outside Damascus. United States president Barack Obama asked Congress to authorize military strikes against Syria for its use of chemical weapons against its own people. But military force was averted. Syria agreed to the destruction of its chemical weapons under a plan proposed by Russia. The international response to the attack proved that many think that more violence—US military attacks—would not prevent future killing of innocent civilians.

We face these incidents of violence again, and again, and again—until we begin to wonder if maybe praying for peace is only part of the picture. Maybe we have to fight for it too.

HOW DO WE FIGHT?

As a Christian, I can't read the headlines without hearing echoes of Jesus' call from the Mount: "Blessed are the peacemakers."

I wonder what it looks like to make peace in Newtown, Connecticut, or in Sanford, Florida. I wonder what it looks like to make peace between bullies and their victims. I wonder what it looks like to make peace between a Middle Eastern regime that would slay

children with nerve gas and religious extremists allied with terrorist organizations. How can we fight for peace in schools, neighborhoods, cities, and a world overwhelmed by violence?

In our FRAMES research, we asked practicing Christians what topics most concern them when it comes to violence. Respondents said the most pressing issues for them are domestic violence (40%); bullying at school (35%); gangs (35%); violence in video games, TV, or movies (33%); and wars in foreign countries (26%). Nearly half of adults (47%) told us they feel less comfortable with violence than they did 10 years ago—among practicing Christians this number is even higher (59%). Among young people, though, there is an admission that they've, perhaps, grown more desensitized to violence. A full 20% of Millennials say

Have you become more or less comfortable with violence in the last 10 years?

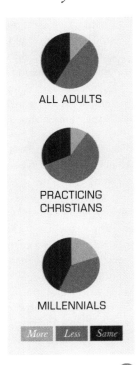

ALL ADULTS

PRACTICING CHRISTIANS

MILLENNIALS

More Less Same

they've grown *more* comfortable with violence in the last decade.

Looking at these statistics, and at the stories recounted above, we can begin to see that violence permeates our culture and our lives at every level.

So, as Christ-followers, how can we fight for peace? And is "fighting" even the right way to think about it? According to the apostle Paul, yes. In his letter to the Ephesians, he urges:

> Be strong in the Lord and in his mighty power. Put on the full armor of God, so that you can take your stand against the devil's schemes. For our struggle is not against flesh and blood, but against the rulers, against the authorities, against the powers of this dark world and against the spiritual forces of evil in the heavenly realms (Ephesians 6:10–12).

Our battle is not against flesh and blood, Paul insists. It's not against other people. Rather, we fight against the darkness of evil and against spiritual powers that keep people bound in cycles of violence and oppression. We fight systemic injustices that marginalize, dehumanize, and disenfranchise people. We fight generational patterns that pass sexual, verbal, or physical abuse from parent to child. We fight prejudices and stereotypes that make us blind to God's image in every single person. We fight the lure of violent images in entertainment, video games, TV shows, and movies with thought and care for others and ourselves. We fight against tribalism and nationalism that justifies attacks on the faceless "other," resisting categories of "us" and "them" that make it easy to inflict suffering on anyone perceived as a threat to our way of life. We fight the impulse in ourselves to hurt, objectify, or use others for our own gain or pleasure.

But how do we fight?

Violence is deeply ingrained in our world, our culture, our families, and even, if we're honest, ourselves. And for peace to happen, we need to fight for it strategically on every single level.

A WORLD AT WAR

"Was that a little kid?" Brandon Bryant demanded when he saw something small skitter across the screen and halt.

"No. It was a dog," his fellow soldier assured him.

But Bryant wasn't convinced and couldn't shake the thought that he had just killed a small child as he sat at the drone command center in a military base in Nevada, far away from his target.

Bryant never thought he could kill a person — let alone 1,626 people, the number of estimated deaths he contributed to over the course of more than a hundred missions. Many things got him to that drone operator's console. High test scores prompted officers to recommend him for the job, telling him he would be like a guy in a James Bond movie. He used multiple screens and a joystick and compared his tasks to playing video games. As he came into the office, pictures of the targeted individuals lined the walls. He would see the faces of terrorists and wonder who was going to die that day.

Today, different images haunt him — heat-sensor outlines of bodies fading as they cooled to the temperature of the concrete below. Civilians, children, sometimes Americans. Bryant, who was ultimately discharged as a result of stress, says he began to feel like a "sociopath" who had "lost respect for life." His trauma continues to follow him in his civilian life.[20] On top of suffering from post-traumatic stress disorder, Bryant is angry Americans seem so removed from the harsh realities of what their military is doing.[21]

Theologians would identify Bryant's condition as "moral injury."[22]

No single soldier is a perpetrator of all violence, but is a product of a larger picture — a military chain of command, a national longing for defense, and a culture too comfortable with violence. In the same way, our own ideas of violence are not totally our own. They are products of our time, our country, our culture, even our churches.

As Christians, we tend to take up one of two positions: We may be proponents of war, imagining God is on our side in our warfare, or we may be so against war that we make no space for the soldiers who have fought. Neither side fully leaves room to make peace. In our own lives and in our churches, we can critically and thoughtfully engage with the ramifications of living in a world at war.

Support soldiers: Many soldiers, like Bryant, express frustration that most Americans have been so removed from the perpetual warfare our country wages that we just don't *care*. Our church communities should be a place where soldiers can find solace and a peace that may seem elusive. In order to understand the violence, we need to listen to soldiers — offering them gratitude for their service and giving them space to grieve and to process their trauma.

Examine the war itself: No matter who might be in office, it's important to remember God is not always on our side. Some of us have had a providential notion of our wars, imagining that since

WAR AND PEACE

Nearly one-third of Americans (32%) cite "foreign wars" as one of their top concerns when it comes to violence. And they remain cautious on topics related to war.

44%
Violent acts sometimes necessary to defend freedom

26%
Patriotic duty to support war

23%
Nuclear weapons necessary for prevention

our nation is majority Christian, then the wars we wage must be done in Jesus' name. We can delude ourselves in thinking our violence is always just.

Understand the theology: Part of the way in which we fight for peace on a global scale is by studying just war theories and pacifist theology.[23] Then we can look at each conflict in the light of what the Bible says and what Jesus teaches.

ACROSS THE TRACKS

I attended Moody Bible Institute in Chicago twenty years ago. A lot has changed in the city, but the lessons I learned about our disparities as a nation remain.

I regularly took care of children for families who live on Chicago's "Gold Coast," a shimmering collection of condominiums and townhouses located near some of the best schools in the city. I walked to the high-rises, feeling safe during the day or evening hours. A uniformed man would check me in and usher me to the elevator. I would take the children to neighborhood parks or to one of the many museums—making sure these children were getting adequate sunshine, exercise, and cultural and intellectual stimulation.

On the other side of the (literal) tracks, life was different. I couldn't walk to the kids' clubs where I—and fellow Moody students—worked in Cabrini Green. Even though it was only a mile away, it was too dangerous, so an old school bus picked us up and transported us. We bumped along the pot-holed road in a rusty bus from one red brick building to the next, picking up excited children for an afternoon filled with basketball and jump ropes.

As I spent each week shuttling from one neighborhood to the next, the effects of violence became clear. On one day, I read to a child whose greatest concern was how well she would do at her piano recital. The next day, a child would worry about what sort of colors he could and couldn't wear in fear of gang retaliation or which patch of grass to avoid stepping on for risk of being shot.

Even as I laughed and enjoyed time with the children from the projects, I knew their futures would be completely different from those who lived less than a mile away. The quality of the children was the same—their charisma, intelligence, and vitality all equally matched—but the geography made all the difference. A child's whole life—her chances of education, success, and opportunities—so scripted by which block she happened to be born on.

Jesse Quam, a fellow student who is now a social worker, helped me understand: "If a rose is in good soil, with sunlight and nourishment, then the flower will flourish. If you put the same rose in the basement without any light, it won't last." Children exposed to violence show signs of depression, anxiety, and low self-esteem.[24] They also become so acclimated to the violence, they learn that it is the only way to solve conflicts.[25]

How could these neighborhoods—so close as to be in the same zip code—be so very different? How could one have the best schools in the city and the other have the worst? Why was one a glimmering tourist destination and the other one of the most crime-ridden neighborhoods in our country?

There are no easy answers to these questions. But research does show us factors that reduce violence in a neighborhood: good education, opportunities for employment, and social connections.[26] These are factors missing from Cabrini Green—and many of our country's poorest areas.

When residents receive quality education, then violence in a neighborhood decreases. As a society, we come together to make sure education is in place, but our public education varies widely in each neighborhood.

When poorer neighborhoods are cut off from economic development that happens in other parts of the city, they become increasingly segregated and severed from social connections and job opportunities.

Additionally, mass incarceration and a punitive culture have dramatically affected social connections in communities of color. Even though crime rates have varied in the last three decades, and are currently at historic lows, the rate of imprisonment has *quintupled*, mostly among African-American men.[27] These young men are often imprisoned during times when they would ordinarily be in the dating pool, settling down in a marriage, or fathering children. And once men have been convicted of a felony, they often cannot get jobs, federal loans for education, subsidized housing, voting rights, or even food stamps. Their futures are cut off. Without any opportunity, violence increases. So the cycle continues.

In our FRAMES research, "gang" violence is one of the biggest concerns for Americans. Indeed, that is the common term for violence in urban, poor contexts, but we would do well to stop and deconstruct that term for a moment. Instead of talking about the context of a problem (such as we would do with wars or domestic violence), we paint a portrait of a certain person, a gang member enacting violence. Instead of looking at the whole picture when it comes to gangs — particularly the ways in which the community is subject to segregation, poor education, lack of opportunities, and mass incarceration — we tend to conjure up a character, instead of looking at the broader issues.

"There is racial coding when we talk about 'gangs,'" Rev. Derrick Weston, the Executive Director of the Pittsburgh Project, told me. "Worries about 'gangs' are worries about dark-skinned young people."

We need to recognize the many variables that contribute to the ways in which our society vilifies men of color.

How can we break down the walls of segregation that keep us from hearing each other's stories? How can we make sure there are good schools and opportunities for all of our neighborhoods? Our churches were central to the civil rights movement and can be vital as we think about community violence. Here are some ideas:

Pulpit swaps and clergy groups: Encourage your pastor to meet with other church leaders in the area. If there is no clergy group available, then host one.

Study Matthew 25: Dedicate time to hearing stories from the soup kitchen, the homeless shelter, and the prison. Ask those representatives what your church can do to fight for peace.

Fight for underfunded schools: Listen to the members of the PTA and teachers from underfunded schools to find out what they need. Give a portion of PTA fundraising to poorer schools or partner with the PTA of another school. (Read more ways to serve local schools in the Barna FRAME *Schools in Crisis* by Nicole Baker Fulgham.)

Learn about the nutrition policies of your state: How are they affecting low-income children? What can you do to make sure the children in your community have healthy meals?

Understand the economic geography of where you live: Look at the economic development of your town. Locate where stores and office spaces are. Locate areas of town that are being neglected. What sort of housing is there? Would it be able to withstand a storm? Does every area have reliable public transportation? Does every area have fresh food or access to toiletries?

Look around at the resources of your church. Are there things you could be doing in order to invest in the economic stimulus in underserved communities? Is there a way in which the church can contribute to the arts or make loans to small businesses?

The shootings at Sandy Hook Elementary School shocked us all. Yet for many people who live and work in poorer communities of color, the death of the children in Newtown reminded them of the violence that daily shakes their neighborhood. Today, children in the United States are twelve times more likely to die from a firearm injury than in twenty-five other industrial nations *combined*.[28] Since 1963, more than 166,000 children and youth have died from guns in our country. This astounding number exceeds the number of US soldiers who died from wars in Vietnam, Afghanistan, and Iraq by threefold.[29]

It can be easy to overlook the disparities that exist in our own cities, especially for people living in abundance. But in order to come to peaceful solutions, we will need to break down the barriers of segregation. As Martin Luther King Jr. reminds us, "There is no easy way to create a world where men and women can live together, where each has his own job and house and where all children receive as much education as their minds can absorb. But if such a world is created in our lifetime, it will be done by ... working toward a world of brotherhood, cooperation, and peace."[30]

BROKEN HOMES

My friend Katie was a teenager when she finally worked up the courage to tell her pastor that her father was abusive. She explained how she had come home one evening, and her father had her sister pinned up against the wall. He was holding her by the neck, screaming obscenities at her. Katie was sure if she had not come home in time, her sister would have been dead.

Katie's pastor didn't believe her. He told Katie she must have misunderstood what she saw. Katie's father had been a leader and generous supporter of the church, and the pastor couldn't imagine Katie was telling the truth.

The abuse continued. Katie begged her mom to leave her dad. Her mom wouldn't leave because she didn't have the resources. Plus, she had gone to a counselor in the church and confided she was afraid for her life. The counselor said she was paranoid.

Katie's mom knew she would lose the respect she had gained in her church as a leader of the women's group. Her church preached strongly against divorce except in cases of abuse, and since no one believed she was actually abused, Katie's mom remained stuck in a violent home, while her children were threatened.

Katie's story is all too common. One out of four women has experienced domestic violence in our country.[31] It is the number one cause of injury for adult women.[32] And nearly one out of every five women has been sexually assaulted. Of course, domestic violence isn't only a women's issue. Eighty percent of domestic violence victims are women, which means 20 percent are men and boys. In fact, as children, boys are more likely to experience harsh physical punishment.[33]

How can we keep Katie's situation from happening in our churches?

Receive their stories: We can begin by trusting and believing the person who tells her story. Being able to testify to abuse can take many years. Many people live with great shame, and they have been told their assessment of their situation is wrong. Having the support of a community who believes them can make a considerable difference in whether a person leaves the abusive situation or not.

Evaluate the ways we tell our own stories: Along with trusting the stories of women who have been abused, we need to think about other ways we unwittingly support violent environments for women and children. Oftentimes in our church communities, we look down on divorce or financial assistance from the government without acknowledging the reality that some women *need* to pursue these options to escape violent homes.

Celebrate survival: Our Scriptures are full of women who have left abusive situations. Listen to the pain of Hagar in her exile. Hear the story of Esther, who was sent to a harem at a young age. Naming the reality of abuse allows women to be able to talk about their own situations. As we study their stories and preach from their perspectives, we celebrate resilience.

We can also celebrate the amazing people who have suffered abuse and found healthy, whole lives at the end of it. Invite the director of the domestic violence shelter in your area to give voice and testimony to the women they have helped.

Support women's shelters: Violence in the home decreases when people have a way out of the abuse. For many people, that means food, shelter, and resources. Find a local women's shelter for your church to support or where you can volunteer. If there is no women's shelter in the community, can your church start one?

Cultivate peaceful homes: Teach children creative ways of nonviolence when they encounter bullying at school or with siblings. Encourage everyone in your family to "use their words" and to dialogue to healthy nonviolent resolutions. Teaching children that violence is never an acceptable response can help to break patterns of abuse and help children recognize abuse when they encounter it.

As we scan American households, we know violence in our homes is real and pervasive: It enters through entertainment, threatens our children in the form of bullying, and poisons generations in endless cycles of abuse.

IN MY DEFENSE

"I have the right to defend myself, even if it requires violence"

All Adults	60%
Male	66%
Practicing Christians	57%
Female	55%
Millennials	52%

FINDING PEACE

A soldier at war. Two children growing up across the tracks but worlds apart. A woman and her daughters ashamed of and terrorized by the abuse in their home.

Global violence. Community violence. Family violence.

These are stories of institutional violence, of systems that oppress and cycles that keep victims trapped. Yet, ultimately, they are also stories of individuals. Of Brandon Bryant the soldier, of me shuffling between those two disparate Chicago neighborhoods, of Katie and her sister and her mother.

Because no matter how distant, vast, or complex the fight for peace can seem, at the center of it—where it must start for each of us—the battle is a personal one.

As a culture we are plagued by anxiety and depression, and many of us carry the scars of trauma within us. Rates of suicide, divorce, and alcoholism have all risen since 1955.[34] In 2000, the *average* child in the United States reported higher rates of depression than children *under psychiatric care* in the 1950s.[35]

I believe we cannot effectively fight for peace beyond ourselves until we begin to fight for peace within ourselves. Each of us is created in God's image with enormous capacity for compassion and care for others. Yet that capacity is diminished and distorted by the violence inflicted on us and the violence we inflict on others. In order to fight for peace in a world that longs so desperately for an alternative to violence, we must allow God to heal and transform us into people at peace and of peace.

This move from the personal to the public reflects the biblical notion of peace. In Hebrew, the language of the Old Testament, the word translated into English as "peace" is *shalom*. This ancient Hebrew word encompasses dimensions of wholeness, economic security, safety, and welfare — not just the absence of war.

Although much of the Old Testament contains extreme examples of war, there are threads of *shalom* woven through the stories that become more prominent with the coming of Jesus. We can see the prophetic longing for peace in Isaiah:

> Many peoples will come and say,
> "Come, let us go up to the mountain of the LORD,
> to the temple of the God of Jacob.
> He will teach us his ways,
> so that we may walk in his paths."
> The law will go out from Zion,
> the word of the LORD from Jerusalem.
> He will judge between the nations
> and will settle disputes for many peoples.
> They will beat their swords into plowshares
> and their spears into pruning hooks.
> Nation will not take up sword against nation,
> nor will they train for war anymore. (Isaiah 2:3 – 4)

Christians breathe that one syllable — *peace* — knowing that when God's Word speaks of peace, its meaning goes far beyond inner, personal contentment to include justice for our families, communities, and world. We might think of peace as the concentric rings of a tree, moving outward from our hearts of *shalom* to our families, neighborhoods, and beyond. But to fight for peace locally and transnationally, we must begin by personally seeking the peace God offers, no matter what violence we have done or what violence has been done to us.

The Process of Peace

Theologian Serene Jones looks to John Calvin as an example of someone who fought for personal peace. As she explains in her book *Trauma and Grace*, Calvin survived life-threatening violence. He fled France in the dead of night, barely escaping imprisonment and execution. Later in Germany, Calvin was asked to minister to a group of French refugees who had fled under similar circumstances. They were afraid to return home, where they would face harassment, maiming, and torture.[36]

Calvin turned to the Psalms, calling them the "anatomy of all parts of the soul." Through his commentaries, we can read how he led himself and his fellow refugees through the stages of Psalmic healing. With Calvin in one hand and more recent texts on trauma in the other, Dr. Jones finds remarkable similarities in the healing process. First, through Psalms of Deliverance (such as Psalm 10), Calvin *establishes safety* in remembering God's merciful acts. Then, through Psalms of Lament (Psalm 22), Calvin leads his flock through a process of *remembering and giving testimony* to their experiences.

Finally, through Psalms of Thanksgiving (Psalm 119), Calvin invites the traumatized to *reintegrate their experiences* into the scope of divine grace.[37]

We can turn to the Psalms and practice these disciplines to fight for peace in our own hearts, minds, and lives. Making meditation a part of our daily routine takes intention, and we may struggle to invest the time while keeping up with a busy life. But the more chaotic our lives, the more we need time for peaceful reflection. Neurologists have shown that meditating even twenty minutes a day can make a measurable difference in the way our brains function.[38] Here are some ways to incorporate Calvin's process of peace into your own life.

Establish safety: Place yourself in an expectant posture. Sitting in a chair might be most comfortable. Uncross your legs and arms. Place your hands on your lap, palms up. Listen to your breathing. Concentrate on how your breath feels on your lips.

Is there a verse of Scripture that reminds you of God's love, protection, or deliverance? Commit it to memory and focus your meditation on the words. For instance, I often meditate on 1 John 4:7: "Dear friends, let us love one another, for love comes from God. Everyone who loves has been born of God and knows God." I shorten it so my prayer matches my breathing. I inhale, "God is love," and imagine the love of God filling my lungs. Then I exhale, "I am born of God," breathing God's love into the air around me.

Remember and give testimony: Many of us fill our lives with noise and busyness in an effort to ignore painful memories. We mistakenly believe we can heal from emotional wounds by pretending they don't exist, but avoiding pain only means it will emerge in destructive ways—like violence against others or ourselves. By acknowledging our wounds and giving voice to pain, we bring the past out of darkness into the light. Following the example of the Psalms of Lament, remember those who have hurt you or those whom you have hurt. We must tell the truth about how we've been hurt so we can be healed.

Give thanks: Make a gratitude list of all for which you are thankful. If you're not sure where to start, begin with the basics: food, shelter, clothing, clean air, and water. Thank God for the hands that harvested your food and sewed your shirt. Envision the many people whose lives are connected to yours, directly and indirectly, and contemplate the back-and-forth effect you have on each other. Thank God for family and friends, those who have mentored and taught you, and children who have opened your heart to deeper love.

Once you have a complete list, offer both the hurts of the past and the blessings of the present to God. The steadfast love of God never ceases; God's mercies never come to an end (see Lamentations 3:22–23). In God's loving hands, your suffering and your blessings are covered by grace and integrated into *shalom*— wholeness. When you acknowledge both violence and grace, and commit them to God's loving care, wholeness is the result.

Close your time of prayer and meditation with the verse of Scripture you focused on at the beginning. Say it a few times as you breathe in and out, conscious that every breath you take is a gift from the Giver of Life.

Praying in this manner not only has a powerful effect on your brain chemistry, but it also affects those around you. Human brains are wired to mimic the emotional responses of others. An angry outburst can make the people around you respond with fear and anger. The same thing happens with peace. When you feel at peace, the people around you are more likely to experience peace.[39]

You may want to begin your "fight for peace" practice by praying for just a few minutes each day. But as the days go by, consider adding time. As you begin to listen to yourself, as you begin to understand what wholeness looks like for your life, attend to the still, small voice of God calling you to fight for peace beyond yourself. When God brings *shalom* to a life that was distorted by violence, peace extends beyond that life alone. As we overcome the wounds of sexual violation, addiction, abuse, bullying, injustice, war, or other manifestations of violence, God equips us to become peacemakers for others. ◆

FIGHTING FOR PEACE

Your Role in a Culture Too Comfortable with Violence

RE/FRAME

BY STEPHAN JOUBERT

The release of Nelson Mandela from prison in 1990 inaugurated a new beginning for South Africa. But the hearts of people sometimes change at a slower pace than the culture. Just ask Pine Pienaar.

Pine, a staunch white Afrikaner, and I grew up together as kids in old South Africa. We'd both seen the toll violence had taken on our homes. I grew up to become a church consultant, and he grew up to become a fighter pilot in the old South African Air Force during the turbulent 1980s. Johnny Walker was his best friend, and his fists were his first line of defense. Even his family said of him, "Pine was one of the most lost people I've ever known."

But then, one day, Pine met Jesus. Pine was just as surprised as everyone who knew him how much Jesus changed his life. Then Jesus surprised Pine again when one morning Pine heard a voice in his heart: "Wash Mariah's feet!"

Mariah was an African domestic worker in Pine's home—and the idea of washing her feet stirred Pine's former racist impulses. Surely this was ridiculous and not a message from God. But the voice persisted. Pine wondered if perhaps God was telling him something. Finally, a third time, Pine heard clearly: "Wash Mariah's feet."

So Pine obeyed. He called Mariah and asked her to take off her shoes. "Why?" she wanted to know. Pine barely knew himself, but he answered, "God spoke to me." In utter amazement, Mariah stared at this bulky, white man on his knees before her. He washed her feet in silence.

Two days later, Mariah broke the silence. "You must come to my church on Sunday," she said.

Now it was Pine's turn to ask why.

"You haven't noticed how slowly I've moved about during the last few months because of the intense pain in my legs. Two days ago, when you washed my feet, I had a letter of resignation in my pocket. I couldn't stand the pain any longer. But then, a miracle happened. After you washed my feet, I could walk again. The pain disappeared. I told my church about the feet washing. They expect you there on Sunday!"

As Pine shared this story with me a few weeks later over coffee, I was deeply touched by the image of this strong ex–air force pilot on his knees before his housekeeper. White and black submitting to each other is a beautiful testimony of God's grace in our country. It was such an incredible story of God's grace and racial reconciliation that I retold it in a column for one of South Africa's daily newspapers.

Little did I know Pine and Mariah's story would soon inspire another foot-washing.

The former minister of police in the Apartheid era, Adriaan Vlok, was one of the most powerful governmental figures in old South Africa. Since then, he has become a committed follower of Christ. When he read Pine and Mariah's story, he knew there was something he must do: He needed to seek restitution and face some of his old opponents—including Frank Chikane. During the Apartheid, Frank was the director general in the office of the state president, and he was also the general secretary of the South African Council of Churches. He was a constant target for the old regime's police because of his public criticism of racial injustices. They even attempted to kill him by trying to put poison on his clothes.

Today, however, the two met on different terms. There, at the headquarters of the South African government in Pretoria, Adriaan asked Frank if he could wash his feet.

At the heart of the old political seat of government, two enemies reconciled in the name of Jesus.

It was a secret meeting, but it wasn't long before word got out that two prominent figures on opposite sides of the political fence had made their peace. The story of Adriaan and Frank's meeting and the foot-washing soon made headlines not only in South Africa, but in newspapers across the globe. Many considered it a sign of reconciliation in a previously divided South Africa.

As Adriaan told me later, he hoped getting down on his knees before a former adversary and asking for forgiveness would demonstrate how God can effect healing and reconciliation—even after so much violence. And it did.

Of course, Adriaan's act of humility did not immediately undo all the effects of the past. He still had to stand in court to answer for some of his police officers' Apartheid crimes, and he received a suspended sentence, which he accepted humbly.

Today, Adriaan still visits groups of the people across South Africa who suffered at the hands of the old regime. He recently attended a meeting in the Cape of a group of people who believe that all perpetrators of Apartheid crimes should be severely punished. Yet after hearing how God changed him, the audience gave him a standing ovation. In traditional African fashion, they asked him to stand in front of the stage while throngs of people walked up to greet and embrace him — a former enemy.

Violence has a way of wrecking a culture — of tearing it apart with hatred and revenge. Yet peace has a way of restoring it — often through surprising means: a white Afrikaner stooping to serve his African housekeeper, two enemies reconciling after years of opposition, and a Savior who makes peace by washing feet. ◆

....

Stephan Joubert is a professor of New Testament at the University of Pretoria and a research associate for theology at the University of Nijmegen in The Netherlands. He is a well-known speaker, preacher, and leadership consultant for many churches and organizations in South Africa and around the world.

AFTER YOU READ

- How might cultivating peace in your own heart and mind spread to your family, community, and even the world? What are some steps you could take now to start these personal practices of peace?

- Will you make different decisions in your engagement with violent entertainment after reading this? Why or why not?

- Which myth of violence most appeals to you: a world without God or a God without the cross? Why would you say that?

- Which story of violence moved you most? The drone operator soldier? The disparity across the tracks? The family too ashamed to escape domestic violence? Notice what moves you and find ways to support victims of that type of violence in your community.

- If you are a parent, what are the areas of violence that most worry you? How can you seek to cultivate a peaceful home and peaceful relationships in your family?

- Name three people you know who need to experience peace. Pray for those people this week. Pray for peace. Fight for peace on their behalf.

SHARE THIS FRAME

Who else needs to know about this trend?
Here are some tools to engage with others.

SHARE THE BOOK

- Any one of your friends can sample a FRAME for FREE.
  Visit zondervan.com/ShareFrames to learn how.

- Know a ministry, church, or small group that would benefit
  from reading this FRAME? Contact your favorite bookseller, or
  visit Zondervan.com/buyframes for bulk purchasing information.

SHARE THE VIDEOS

- See videos for all 9 FRAMES on barnaframes.com and use
  the share links to post them on your social networks and share
  them with friends.

SHARE ON FACEBOOK

- Like facebook.com/barnaframes and be the first to see new
  videos, discounts, and updates from the Barna FRAMES team.

SHARE ON TWITTER

- Start following @barnaframes and stay current with the
  trends that are influencing and changing our culture.

- Join the conversation and include #barnaframes whenever
  you post a FRAMES related idea or culture-shaping trend.

SHARE ON INSTAGRAM

- Follow instagram.com/barnaframes for sharable visual
  posts and infographics that will keep you in the know.

Barna Group

ZONDERVAN°

ABOUT THE RESEARCH

FRAMES started with the idea that people need simple, clear ideas to live more meaningful lives in the midst of increasingly complex times. To help make sense of culture, each FRAME includes major public-opinion studies conducted by Barna Group.

If you're into the details, the research behind the *Fighting for Peace* FRAME included 1,000 surveys conducted among a representative sample of adults over the age of 18 living in the United States and included an oversample of 404 interviews completed by 18- to 29-year-olds. This survey was conducted from June 25, 2013, through July 1, 2013. The sampling error for both surveys is plus or minus 3 percentage points, at the 95% confidence level.

If you're really into the research details, find more at www.barnaframes.com.

ABOUT BARNA GROUP

In its thirty-year history, Barna Group has conducted more than one million interviews over the course of hundreds of studies and has become a go-to source for insights about faith and culture. Currently led by David Kinnaman, Barna Group's vision is to provide people with credible knowledge and clear thinking, enabling them to navigate a complex and changing culture. The company was started by George and Nancy Barna in 1984.

Barna Group has worked with thousands of businesses, nonprofit organizations, and churches across the country, including many Protestant and Catholic congregations and denominations. Some of its clients have included the American Bible Society, CARE, Compassion, Easter Seals, Habitat for Humanity, NBC Universal, the Salvation Army, Walden Media, the ONE Campaign, SONY, Thrivent, US AID, and World Vision.

The firm's studies are frequently used in sermons and talks. And its public-opinion research is often quoted in major media outlets, such as *CNN*, *USA Today*, the *Wall Street Journal*, Fox News, *Chicago Tribune*, the *Huffington Post*, the *New York Times*, *Dallas Morning News*, and the *Los Angeles Times*.

Learn more about Barna Group at www.barna.org.

THANKS

Even small books take enormous effort.

First, thanks go to Carol Howard Merritt and Tyler Wigg-Stevenson for their insightful work on this FRAME—offering their perspectives, experiences, and considerable knowledge to create what we pray is a prophetic challenge to a culture surrounded by violence—both seen and unseen.

We are also incredibly grateful for the thoughtful contribution of Stephan Joubert, who has been in the trenches fighting for peace for decades.

Next, Barna Group gratefully acknowledges the efforts of the team at HarperCollins Christian Publishing, especially Chip Brown and Melinda Bouma for catching the vision from the get-go. Others at HarperCollins who have made huge contributions include Jennifer Keller, Kate Mulvaney, Mark Sheeres, and Shari Vanden Berg.

The FRAMES team at Barna Group consists of Elaina Buffon, Bill Denzel, Traci Hochmuth, Pam Jacob, Clint Jenkin, Robert Jewe, David Kinnaman, Jill Kinnaman, Elaine Klautzsch, Stephanie Smith, and Roxanne Stone. Bill and Stephanie consistently made magic out of thin air. Clint and Traci brought the research to life—along with thoughtful analysis from Ken Chitwood. And Roxanne deserves massive credit as a shaping force on FRAMES. Amy Duty did heroic work on FRAMES designs, from cover to infographics.

Finally, others who have had a huge role in bringing FRAMES to life include Brad Abare, Justin Bell, Jean Bloom, Patrick Dodd, Ashley Emert, Grant England, Esther Fedorkevich, Josh Franer, Jane Haradine, Aly Hawkins, Kelly Hughes, Steve McBeth, Geof Morin, Jesse Oxford, Beth Shagene, and Santino Stoner.

Many thanks!

NOTES

1. Committee on the Judiciary, United States Senate, 102nd Congress, "Violence Against Women, A Majority Staff Report," October 1992, 3.

2. Joseph Heller, *Catch 22* (New York: Simon & Schuster Paperbacks, 2004), 440.

3. Rob Reiner, Director, *A Few Good Men*, 1992.

4. Walter Wink, "Facing the Myth of Redemptive Violence," *Ekklesia: A New Way of Thinking*, May 21, 2012, http://www.ekklesia.co.uk/content/cpt/article_060823wink.shtml. See also Wink's "powers" trilogy: *Naming the Powers, Engaging the Powers,* and *Unmasking the Powers*, all from Fortress Press.

5. Wink, "Facing the Myth of Redemptive Violence."

6. Stephen P. Wink and Walter Wink, "Domination, Justice, and the Cult of Violence," *Saint Louis University Law Journal* 38, January 1, 1993, 341–78.

7. Wink, "Facing the Myth of Redemptive Violence."

8. Rene Lynch, "'DJesus Uncrossed': Most Blasphemous skit in 'SNL' History?" *Los Angeles Times*, February 18, 2013, http://herocomplex.latimes.com/movies/djesus-uncrosse-snl-skit-guilty-of-blasphemy/.

9. Wink, "Facing the Myth of Redemptive Violence."

10. Per capita, the United States spends less than half of what South Korea or the Netherlands (for example) does on video games, many of which are violent, but the United States has a gun murder rate more than twelve times higher than either country. Moreover, while video game sales have doubled since the mid-1990s, the number of violent youth offenders has plummeted in the same period. Add to this the global popularity of American film and music, and it gets difficult to pin the blame for violent actions on the entertainment we consume. See also: Erik Kain, "The Truth About Video Games and Gun Violence," *Mother Jones*, June 11, 2013, http://www.motherjones.com/politics/2013/06/video-games-violence-guns-explainer; Max Fisher, "Ten-Country Comparison Suggests There's Little or No Link Between Video Games and Gun Murders," *The Washington Post*, December 17, 2012, http://www.washingtonpost.com/blogs/worldviews/wp/2012/12/17/ten-country-comparison-suggests-theres-little-or-no-link-between-video-games-and-gun-murders/.

11. Erik Kain, "Do Games Like 'Grand Theft Auto V' Cause Real-World

Violence?," *Forbes*, September 18, 2013, http://www.forbes.com/sites/
erikkain/2013/09/18/do-games-like-grand-theft-auto-v-cause-real
-world-violence/.

12. Augustine of Hippo, *Confessions and Enchiridion*, trans. Albert C.
Outler (Grand Rapids, MI: Christian Classics Ethereal Library, n.d.), 6.8,
http://www.ccel.org/ccel/augustine/confessions. Emphasis mine.

13. http://avpusa.org.

14. David P. Gushee, *Righteous Gentiles of the Holocaust: Genocide and
Moral Obligation* (St. Paul, MN: Paragon House, 2003).

15. Georges Bataille, *Inner Experience* (New York: SUNY Press, 1988),
120.

16. Andy Crouch, *Playing God: Redeeming the Gift of Power* (Downers
Grove, IL: InterVarsity Press, 2013).

17. Jonathan Hill, *Zondervan Handbook to the History of Christianity*
(Grand Rapids, MI: Zondervan, 2006), 46.

18. There are a number of resources for churches wanting to invest in
this kind of care. To learn more, see the work of the Soul Repair Center
at Brite Divinity School, which focuses on recovery from "moral injury"
sustained in violent conflict: http://www.brite.edu/soulrepair/. For another
model, see Reboot Combat Recovery: http://www.rebootrecovery.com/.
The Centurion's Guild supports military service members in exercising the
rights of conscience: https://www.facebook.com/CenturionsGuild.

19. John Sobrino SJ, *Christology at the Crossroads: A Latin American
Approach* (New York: Orbis, 1976), 201–2.

20. Robert Johnson, " 'Did We Just Kill a Kid?' Six Words That Ended
a US Drone Pilot's Career," *Business Insider*, Dec. 17, 2012.

21. Richard Engel, "Former drone operator says he's haunted by his part in
more than 1,600 deaths," NBC News, June 6, 2013, http://investigations
.nbcnews.com/_news/2013/06/06/18787450-former-drone-operator-says
-hes-haunted-by-his-part-in-more-than-1600-deaths?lite.

22. Samuel Freedman, "Tending to Veterans' Afflictions of the Soul," *New
York Times*, January 11, 2013. The story explains how theologian Rita
Nakashima Brock works with veterans, tending to "moral injuries."

23. "War," *Stanford Encyclopedia of Philosophy*. First published Feb. 4,
2000; substantive revision, July 28, 2005, http://plato.stanford.edu/
entries/war/.

24. Susan FitzGerald, " 'Crack baby' study ends with unexpected but clear
results," *Philadelphia Inquirer*, July 22, 2013.

25. Marian Wright Edelman, "Numb — Spiritually Dead — Nation,"
Huffington Post Politics, May, 24, 2013, http://www.huffingtonpost.com/
marian-wright-edelman/numb---spiritually-dead_b_3333658.html.

26. Michele Alexander, *The New Jim Crow: Mass Incarceration in the Age of Colorblindness* (New York: The New Press, 2010).

27. Alexander, *The New Jim Crow*, 101. Also see "Michelle Alexander, author of *The New Jim Crow*—2013 George E. Kent Lecture," http://www.youtube.com/watch?v=Gln1JwDUI64.

28. James E. Atwood, *America and Its Guns* (Eugene, OR: Cascade Books, 2012), 5.

29. Edelman, "Numb—Spiritually Dead."

30. James M. Washington, editor, *A Testament of Hope: The Essential Writings and Speeches of Martin Luther King, Jr.* (San Francisco: Harper San Francisco, 1986), 61.

31. Committee on the Judiciary, United States Senate, 102nd Congress, "Violence Against Women, A Majority Staff Report," October 1992, 3.

32. Roni Caryn Rabin, "Nearly 1 in 5 Women in U.S. Survey Say They Have Been Sexually Assaulted," *The New York Times*, December 14, 2011.

33. Tracie O. Afifi, Natalie P. Mota, Patricia Dasiewicz, Harriet L. MacMillan, and Jitender Sareen, "Physical Punishment and Mental Disorders: Results from a Nationally Representative US Sample," *Pediatrics: Official Journal of the American Academy of Pediatrics*, July 2, 2012.

34. This is not to say we were entirely better off 60 years ago. I am thrilled at how far we have come with civil rights and women's rights. It is simply a marker in order to notice the trend of depression is on the rise.

35. Bill McKibben, *Deep Economy: The Wealth of Communities and Our Durable Future* (New York: Times Books, 2007), 36.

36. Serene Jones, *Trauma and Grace: Theology in a Ruptured World* (Louisville: Westminster John Knox, 2009), 47.

37. Ibid.

38. Andrew Newberg, M.D., and Mark Robert Waldman, *How God Changes Your Brain: Breakthrough Findings from a Leading Neuroscientist* (New York: Ballantine Books, 2009), 20, 43–44.

39. Newberg and Waldman, *How God Changes Your Brain*, 141.